RURAL DEVELOPMENT TRENDS IN NIGERIA

Ugwuaku Ogechukwu Virginia

Ugwuaku Ogechukwu Virginia

Copyright © 2021 Ugwuaku Ogechukwu Virginia

All rights reserved

The characters and events portrayed in this book are fictitious. Any similarity to real persons, living or dead, is coincidental and not intended by the author.

No part of this book may be reproduced, or stored in a retrieval system, or transmitted in any form or by any means, electronic, mechanical, photocopying, recording, or otherwise, without express written permission of the publisher.

ISBN: 9798503594546

Cover design by: Art Painter
Library of Congress Control Number: 2018675309
Printed in the United States of America

This work is dedicated to the Almighty God and to all my affiliate loved ones.

CONTENTS

Title Page

Copyright

Dedication

Introduction

Preface

Concept of Rural Development — 1

Various Rural Development Approaches — 5

Governments' Experiences in Rural Development — 8

Problems Affecting Rural Development in Nigeria — 20

The Way Forward — 23

Conclusion — 27

References — 29

About The Author — 33

Books By This Author — 35

INTRODUCTION

Generally, development is seen as process by which man increases or maximizes his control and use of the material resources with which nature has endowed him and his environment. Afigbo (1991) affirmed that development consists of five main ingredients: increasing material wealth for the use of individuals and the modern collectivity known as the nation; eliminating unemployment; eliminating poverty and want; eliminating inequality, and increasing the general availability of labour-saving devices. Development, from its inception, is a kind of totalistic movement and rural development is not an exception. Therefore, rural development is a multi-dimensional process by which the productivity, income and welfare, in terms of health, nutrition, education and other features of satisfactory life of rural people can be improved upon or transformed. According to Igbokwe and Ajala (1995), the earliest attempt at rural development during the colonial era took the form of community development, and later agricultural extension. The community development approach emphasized self-help to improve health, nutrition and community welfare, whereas the agricultural extension approach was concerned with improving the agricultural productivity. The goal of both programmes ultimately was to produce primary products for the feeding of European industries.

The early years of Nigeria's independence witnessed colossal concentration of development efforts on the modern sector of the economy to the exclusion of investment in the rural economic base. Therefore, the problem has been how to make rural development sustainable. Towards this end, a number of development approaches have been pursued by the various governments in Nigeria. These consist mainly in the establishment of projects, programmes, and capacity-building institutions. One shortcoming of these efforts is the limited local community participation in problem identification, project prioritization, design, preparation and implementation. Suffice it to state that most of these development approaches are elitist and urban-biased, such that the rural areas are often given lip attention in virtually all ramifications of modernization process. The rural sector is still largely characterized by absence of basic human needs and underdevelopment in agricultural and non-agricultural activities (Williams, 1994). In line with the fore-going, Diejomaoh in Ayichi (1995) asserted that rural development is a process of not only increasing the level of per capita income in the rural areas but also the standard of living of the rural population measured by food and nutrition level, health, education, housing, recreation and security. It is therefore the process of rural modernization and the monetization of the rural society leading to its transition from traditional isolation to integration with the national economy.

PREFACE

The study is on the reflections of rural development in Nigeria. Rural development is the integrated approach to food production as well as physical, social and institutional infrastructural provisions with an ultimate goal of bringing about both quantitative and qualitative changes which result in improved living standard of the rural population. Embarking on rural development is very important considering the fact that more than two-third of the Nigeria's population are living in rural areas, and they experience a lot of misery, poverty, morbidity and under-development. Reflection on the Nigerian Government experiences in rural development showed that not much has been achieved even before and after independence. There exists a sharp contrast between policy formulation and its implementation. The resultant effect becomes more hardship and poor standard of living among the rural dwellers. This paper also x-rayed the various approaches to rural development by highlighting the strengths and weaknesses of each. The government's failure in the various rural development strategies emanated from lack of national philosophical base, lack of cohesive identity, inadequate community participation, lack of grassroots planning and inability of the government to optimize local resources, among other problems. Finally, the study postulated that there should be adequate supply of infrastructural facilities, small and medium-scale industries and political empowerment of the rural people by government. These measures would go a long way improving their living conditions.

CONCEPT OF RURAL DEVELOPMENT

Rural Development is part of general development that embraces a large segment of those in great need in the rural sector. Hunter (1964) was among the earliest to use the expression Rural Development which he considered as the "starting point of development" characterized by subsistence. World Bank in Ekpo and Olaniyi (1995) defined rural development as a process through which rural poverty is alleviated by sustained increases in the productivity and incomes of low-income rural dwellers and households. This definition is defective as it dwelt majorly on the economic growth, which is just an aspect of development. Taking into cognizance, the economic growth and social upliftment as aspects of development, Ijere (1990) regarded rural development, as the process of increasing the per capita income and the quality of life of the rural dweller to enable him become prime mover of his own destiny. Obinne in Ogidefa (2010) perceived rural development to involve creating and widening opportunities for (rural) individuals to realize full potential through education and share in decision and action which affect their lives. He also viewed it as efforts to increase rural output and create employment opportunities and root out fundamental (or extreme) cases of poverty, diseases and ignorance.

Therefore, combining all the essential elements of development, Rural Development can be described as the integrated approach to food production as well as physical, social and institutional infrastructural provisions with an ultimate goal of bringing about both quantitative and qualitative changes which result in improved living standard of the rural population. It therefore, infers that agricultural production (development) is a component of rural development as more than two-third of Nigeria's 150 million citizens are farmers. They live in an estimated 97,000 rural communities. Their lives are characterized by misery, poverty, morbidity and under-development (Ekpo&Olaniyi, 1995). Hence, it has been widely recognized that the rural areas and people are characterized by the following: general poverty trap, low income and investment ratchet, underutilized and/or unutilized natural resources, rapidly increasing population, under-employment and/or disguised employment, low productivity, especially of labour, low and traditional technology, limited enterprise or entrepreneurship, high level of illiteracy, ignorance, disease and malnutrition, near absence of social and physical infrastructures (like all-season roads, potable water, electricity, good schools, health centres, etc.), and political powerlessness, gullibility and level of general vulnerability (Lele&Adu-Nyako, 1991: 1 – 29).

 Rural development has scope that is broad and elastic, and it depends on the interaction of many forces such as the objectives of the programme, the availability of resources for planning and implementation, etc. In developing countries, such as Nigeria, rural development projects will include agricultural set-up projects, rural water supply projects, rural electrification projects, rural feeder-road and maintenance projects, rural health and disease control projects, rural education and Adult education campaign, rural telecommunication system, and rural industrialization. Based on the scope of rural development (as the improvement of the total welfare of the rural low-income people), the following objectives of rural development evolved:

 (i) to have greater commitment of the resources to the rural areas in terms of budgeting allocation and ac-

tual expenditure.
(ii) to ensure popular participation of the rural people in the identification of priorities, planning of programmes as well as their implementation.
(iii) to lay greater emphasis on the use of total resources and promotion of local skills.
(iv) to expand and improve on rural infrastructure such as roads, markets stalls, electricity, water and storage facilities.
(v) to maintain political and social stability
(vi) to create rural employment opportunities
(vii) to increase commodity out-put and production and subsequently increase food and food supply as well as rural farm incomes

From the objectives of the rural development in Nigeria, Ijere (1990) postulated that the underlying principles of rural development are as follows:

i. The leaders and policy-makers should be committed to the philosophy of rural development for the improvement of the rural sector.

ii. There should be total community involvement in rural development. To ensure this, rural development organizers should delegate powers to local leaders at all levels of the population who should account for the exercise of that power. Also, a more suitable community participation approach using the people's institutions and leaders is imperative.

iii. Incentives and motivation should be built into the rural development system. These could be in form of citations, honourable mentions, honorary titles and prizes, competition between villages, towns and local government areas, organizing rural development day to select the best farmers, cleanest communities, accident-free communities, etc.

iv. All aspects of the peoples life should be affected by the rural development schemes to allow for even development.

v. A core of local leadership should be built-up to sustain the rural development effort. There should be a standing development planning committee in every community from which such persons can be mobilized.

vi. There should be development of appropriate skills (human capital development) as well as implementation capacity to sustain new technologies and improvement of social welfare.

vii. Rural development programmes should utilize the cultural values and practices of the people. It makesthe scheme understandable and meaningful. Indigenous institutions such as age grades; youth organizations, clubs and town unions should be used in reaching the people and in mobilizing latent energies (pp. 66–67).

VARIOUS RURAL DEVELOPMENT APPROACHES

The overall aim of rural development efforts is geared towards the improvement of the lives of the rural population. However, several approaches aimed at arresting the ugly under-development situation in rural areas have been put forward. According to Ijere (1990: 52 – 54), they include the following:

1. **Growth Pole Centre Model:** This model is also known as "Growth Point Model". The model involves the development of a few strategic towns, communities and industries likely to activate other sectors. The model focuses attention on the development of few towns leading to the neglect of the rural areas.

2. **The "Big Push" Policy:** This approach is similar to the growth pole centre model except that it is more concentrated. It takes a few sub-sectors and expends most of the resources on them in the hope that in the long run, their multiplier effect will salvage the whole economy. The flaw in this model is that "in the long run" is not a specific period.

3. **The Selective Approach:** This model/approach involves the selection of certain sectors for development based on economic,

political, social or religious grounds, which may not necessarily be related or inter-connected.

4. The Protectionist Approach: In this approach, the government carries out the development process on behalf of the people believing that it knows everything and that the people are not yet ripe to participate, in the management of their own affairs.

5. The Top-down Approach: It is also called the Top-bottom approach. It is a strategy based on passing down to the poor certain policies and directives from the governing bureaucracy. This type of rural development approach requires force to maintain and sustain it.

6. The Decentralized Territorial Approach: This approach centres on the dispersal of benefits to the rural area. It has minimum linkage with the city but with settlements of various sizes to act as service and market centres. The defect in this approach is the undue fear of towns being exploitative and parasitic, and the consideration that size alone could determine the performance of a settlement.

7. The "Laissez-faire" Policy: In this model, the authorities use the role of thumb, past experience, hind-sight and the free market mechanism to manage the economy, with the hope that the invisible hand of God would ensure optimum happiness for everybody.

8. The Key Settlement Strategy: This model is closely related to growth pole centre model except that its focus is on settlement. It assumes a focal point for a given rural area, and the concentration of all rural development resources in such a settlement. This in turn will serve other regions through its network of roads and communication. This model requires a long time to mature, and therefore it is more expensive.

9. The Adaptive Approach: It is a combination of selective approach and Laissez-faire policy and any other approach. It gives the people the opportunity to decide on their own lives, sometimes, under the guidance of the government.

10. The "Bottom-Up" Approach: It is also called Bottom-top approach or Rurism strategy. This approach implies that development starts with the people. It is a new political development strategy. Rurism is a coherent national and social-value system in which human and material resources are mobilized and allocated from the lower echelon of the economic and social strata to the top. It is free from any foreign ideology and infection. It promotes self-reliance, self-consciousness into balanced development of human and material resources. It is the ideal approach. However, it is costly and rather slow.

GOVERNMENTS' EXPERIENCES IN RURAL DEVELOPMENT

There has been a lot of rhetoric about the pattern of life and living in the rural areas. The rhetoric ranges from romanticized account of pastoral beauty at the serenity of living found in rural areas. To this, Nigeria is not an exception. There has been a lot of misunderstanding about what rural development is. The services and misunderstanding about rural areas is evident in the various governmental programmes that have been tossed around. The expectations of government in rural development are viewed from two perspectives:

i.   Pre-lndependence Experience
ii. Post-Independence Experience

A. Pre-Independence Experience in Rural Development

During the colonial era, roads and railway lines were constructed up and across the country, in the name of and ostensibly for the development of rural areas. Perhaps, they were done to open up the hinterland for civilization. However, the real reason for such constructions was to enable the colonialists and the imperialists to tap and evacuate our agricultural products such as groundnuts, cocoa, cotton, and palm produce. In the rural areas within this era, agricultural mechanization was introduced to increase the hectares of food production for export; and also for the maximization and exploitation of the rural areas. The objective of the development of the rural areas during this period is secondary and not of primary objective. Though most appropriate, the colonial administration did not use the village, town and clan unions for purposes of rural development because of fear that they might constitute hotbeds of political propaganda. Rather, they became useful in tax collections and rallies on Empire Days.

B. Post-Independence Experience in Rural Development

After independence, the rhetoric and lip service were even thicker. This time, indigenous politicians and bureaucrats do it and many of who were themselves emigrates from rural areas. The period witnessed colossal concentration of development efforts on the modern sector of the economy to the exclusion of investment in the rural economic base. Government intervention in rural transformation then were in response to lifting urban pressures emanating from rural neglect and improving export commodity earnings (Igbokwe&Ajala, 1995). They now cart away the nation's wealth for personal savings abroad for security. They started their attack on rural development through the institution of marketing and commodity board. The aim of the marketing board was to help the farmers sell their produce in the world market to the advantage of the farmers, and also to cushion the effects of price fall in the world market. It is now known that not only were the farmers grossly underpaid from their labour, but even the money got from their taxes and levies which supposed to be reserved to cushion the price effects were diverted into other uses. Example of such diversion was the construction of prestigious projects like the Cocoa House at Ibadan. In such way, the exploitative attitudes of the urban elites towards the rural areas continued unabated. The consequences of all these are hunger and famine that have hunted our country forcing the government to import all the foodstuffs that we needed. So, it became more profitable and more sensible to remain in cities even as unemployed than to be enslaved in the rural areas just to feed the nation.

In the 1970s, there was a renewed effort in what was called rural development. The main idea was actually a desperate effort to ensure adequate food supply for the nation, especially for the parasitic urbanites. The efforts really served the needs of the cities through which the best and the choicest food produced were carted away by the middle men who had bought them at ridiculously low prices from the original producers. The policy was in practice, and implementation was exploitative and impoverished to the rural areas because they were aimed at enhancement of food and crop production only. Billions of Naira has been spent on rural development projects, yet the conditions of the rural inhabitants continued to be poorer, abject and pitiable or miserable. This is because the projects were not aimed at developing the rural people, and where they happened to contribute to the development, such contributions were secondary and distant. However, Government of various regimes employed some strategies aimed at developing the rural areas in Nigeria. Some of the tried strategies are:

1. The National Accelerated Food Production Project (NAFPP). This project was launched in 1973 and it continued until 1976 when it was replaced by the Operation Feed the Nation Programme. It was an impact-making agricultural strategy to increase food production in specific areas and sub-sectors of the agricultural economy. NAFPP relied heavily on the cooperative approach as well as on technical assistance for its success. The scheme was a well-conceived and guided change programme for rural development, especially in the area of food production.

2. Operation Feed the Nation. This programme was launched in 1976 by the then Head of State of Nigeria. Lt. Gen. OlusegunObasanjo. It was designed to awaken in the generality of Nigerians the advantages of the agricultural occupation, especially, those living in the rural areas. The objectives of the Operation Feed the

Nation were as follows:

i. to mobilize the nation towards self-sufficiency and self-reliance in food production.

ii. to encourage the sector of the community relying heavily on food purchase to grow their own food.

iii. to encourage general pride in agriculture.

iv. to encourage balanced nutritional feeding and thereby produce a healthy nation.

The Operation Feed the Nation was not specifically a rural development strategy, but the rural areas benefited through inputs and professional advice. However, Osuntogun and Olufokunbi (1986) observed that the Operation Feed the Nation rather than solving food problems created opportunities for the ruling class to appropriate national funds. They were appointed Board members as well as given fat contracts.

3. The Agricultural Development Projects (ADP). The projects commenced in Nigeria in 1975. The World Bank, the Federal and State Governments jointly own them. The ultimate objective of the Agricultural Development Projects system was to raise productivity, increase farm output, income and standard of living of the rural people. The emphasis was on the promotion of small-scale autonomous projects operated by a multi-disciplinary management unit. Using the cooperative approach, they tackled many aspects of agriculture, which include production, marketing, infrastructure and training. The problem with the Agricultural Development Projects was that they used a mixture of settlement and big-push approaches. As such, their heavy capitalization prevented their adoption by government and organizations.

4. The River-BasinDevelopment Authority (RBDA). It was first launched in 1962, expanded in 1976 and further expanded in 1983. However, it was revised and curtailed between 1984 and 1986. The declared aim of the authority was to make the nation self-sufficient in food production and to uplift the socio-economic standard of the rural dwellers. Accordingly, Federal Republic of

Nigeria (1981) reported that government provided in the Third National Development Plan huge sum of money to develop the main rivers of the country to benefit agriculture and rural development. However, the activities of the authority showed that the development philosophywas still the trickle-down approach as rural development was not a serious issue in the objectives of the River-Basin Development Authority, which included:

i. to undertake comprehensive development, both surface and underground water resources for multi-purpose use.

ii. to undertake scheme for the control of flood, and erosion, and for the water-shed management including afforestation.

iii. to construct and maintain dams, dykes, wells, bore-holes, irrigations and drainage systems.

iv. to provide water from reservoir and lakes for irrigation purposes to farmers and recognized associations, as well as for urban water supply scheme.

v. to control pollution in rivers, lakes, lagoons, and creeks.

All the activities of the authorities were geared at the development of material things, objects and gadgets, and not at the development of the people as persons. The activities were only done for the people, not with the people and by the people. Also, the impact of the RBAs was limited due to conflicting policy changes and lack of management know-how. According to Okorie and Umezurike (1990), the RBDAs diverted from their traditional roles to that of food production. Moreover, the increasing cost of running them due to huge capital investment led to several policy adjustments.

5. Green Revolution. It is a crash programme launched in 1980 by AlhajiShehuShagari's Administration. It was aimed at boasting food production in a bid to provide food to every Nigerian. The objectives of Green Revolution include:

➢ to make the country self-sufficient in food production within 5 years.

➢ to return the country to its pre-eminent crop production

stage within 7 years.

Unfortunately, it failed because the same government that instituted Green Revolution with the aim of making Nigeria self-sufficient as at 1985, embarked on a large-scale importation of rice from India and America, and essential food items for survival and sustenance (Otoghagua, 1999). Again, the sole intention of the programme was food and crop production so that the physical hunger of urban areas and the impoverished foreign exchange account of the government might be replenished. The presumption was that once agriculture was improved, and the yields per acre were increased, the peasant farmers who constitute the major bulk of the producers would automatically have their economic and social standard improved. It is very clear that there was no mention of how to channel the money back, extracted from the rural areas to develop the area.

6. Directorate for Food, Roads and Rural Infrastructure (DFRRI). The directorate was one of the numerous programmes that were instituted by the then President of Nigeria, Gen. Ibrahim BadamosuBabangida in 1985. It was a kind of home-grown social dimensions of Adjustment project for Nigeria. According to Ekpo and Olaniyi (1995), DFRRI has the following objectives:

i. to improve the quality of life and standard of living of the majority of the people in the rural areas by:
   - improving greatly the quality, value and nutritional balance of their food intake;
   - raising the quality of rural housing, as well as the general living and working environment in the rural areas;
   - improving the health condition of the rural people;
   - creating greater opportunities for human development and employment; especially self-employment and invariably enhancing rural income levels;
   - making it possible to have a progressively wider range and variety of goods and services to be produced and consumed by the rural people themselves as well as for exchange;

ii. to utilize the enormous resources of the rural areas to lay a solid foundation for the security, socio-cultural, political and economic growth and development activities of the rural areas;

iii. to ensure a deeply-rooted self-sustaining development process based on effectively mobilized mass participation, beginning from the grass roots and spreading thereafter to the wider economy (p. 138).

The Nigeria's DFRRI can be perceived as a kind of integrated rural development strategy. Its activities can be grouped into the following broad areas: Provision of Economic and Social Infrastructures, Production of Agricultural Inputs, Development and Dissemination of Improved Technology to enhance agricultural and rural housing and Mobilization for Mass Participation in rural development.

a. Provision of Economic and Social Infrastructures: DFRRI developed rural access roads. Government surveys indicated that 60, 000km of ruralfeeder roads were either constructed or rehabilitated under the first phase which was completed in 1987. In 1990, a total of 30,724.34km of rural feeder roads were completed and accepted as having met the required specifications under the second phase of the project. Another 55,576.24km of rural roads were constructed in 1991. However, in 1992, a total of 85,592.82km of rural feeder roads were completed, inspected and accepted as can be found on table I below. Another important infrastructure on which DFRRl's resources were concentrated was rural electrification. The first phase took off in 1987. Two model villages in each local government area of the country were selected for the project so as to serve as reference points in rural development in the country. By 1989, 142 electricity projects were completed in phase 1. In 1990, 114 communities in 11 states were provided with electricity. In 1991, 325 communities were supplied with electricity, and another 506 communities benefited in 1992. Also, on water supply to rural communities, 4, 000 wells/boreholes were reported to have been sunk by 1989. Another I,

291; 11, 310 and 18, 680 wells and boreholes were sunk in 1990, 1991 and 1992, respectively (Ekpo&Olaniyi, 1995).

Table 1: DFRRI's Completed Projects on Economic and Social Infrastructures

Year	Amount Allocated (₦ Million)	Feeder Roads (km)	Rural Electricity (No. of communities)	Boreholes/ wells
1986	500	—	—	—
1987	400	60, 000	—	—
1988	500	30, 000	—	—
1989	300	30, 000	142	4, 000
1990	300	30, 728.34	114	1, 291
1991	152.3	55, 576.24	325	11, 310
1992	250	85, 592.82	506	18, 680
Source: DFRRI Press Briefing (1992).				

b. Production of Agricultural Inputs: With respect to DFRRI's production activities, two special programmes for cultivating 50 million fruit trees and producing improved seeds or mass distribution were launched in 1986. In 1987, various research institutes were engaged in the Directorate's seeds multiplication and distribution, livestock, horticulture and aquaculture development programmes. The end of 1987 marked a total production of 3,624 tonnes of assorted breeder/foundation seeds for livestock. In 1990, 1, 633 tonnes of seeds of arable crops, 4, 598 million oil palm seedlings and 294,072 tonnes of groundnut seeds were distributed to farmers. Aqua culture also increased through the production of 2, 666 million fish fingerlings. In 1991, the achievements improved some 4, 033.13 tonnes of improved seeds. 17, 112 million seedlings, 2, 666 million fingerlings and 14, 529 tonnes of fodder seeds were produced and distributed to farmers. In 1992, 846, 224 fruit seedlings for horticulture, 5, 726.13 tonnes of arable crops seeds and 3, 466 million fingerlings were produced and distributed to farmers as shown on table 2 below.

Table 2: DFRRI's Supply of Agricultural Inputs

Year	Arable crops (tonnes)	Oil palm (million)	Groundnuts (tonnes)	Fodder seeds (tonnes)	Horticulture (tonnes)	Fish (million)
1987	—	—	—	3, 624	—	—
1988	—	—	—	—	—	—
1989	—	—	—	—	—	—
1990	1, 633	4, 598	294, 072	—	—	2.67
1991	4, 033.13	17, 112	—	14, 529	—	2.67
1992	5, 726.13	—	—	—	846, 224	3.47

Source: Adopted and modified from Ekpo and Olaniyi (1995).

c. Development and Dissemination of Improved Technology: Another important project embarked upon by DFRRI was its collaboration with Nigerian Building and Road Research Institute

(NBRRI), Project Development Agency (PRODA) and Bida Polytechnic on research into the ways of using local raw materials, and improving local technology for constructing houses in rural areas, the rural housing unit of the Directorate trained about 250 technical personnel from all the states; on how to use locally available raw materials and technology for building houses. In 1992, a total of 8, 024 technical extension workers were engaged in various communities to boost rural housing. The number of rural farmers who were able to go to farm in motorized vehicles increased by 23.6 per cent of the rural population between 1986 and 1993, and 31.4% of the rural dwellers had access to new health facilities built during the periods.

d. Mobilization for Mass Participation: DFRRI encouraged and assisted in the formation of community development associations (CDAs) and community banks (which have metamorphosed into microfinance banks). The CDAs became very significant in rural development. They identified projects, assisted DFRRI, and mobilized the rural dwellers to partake in modernizing their domain. Between 1989 and 1991, a total of 8,108 CDAs were registered. Also, community banks were established in almost all the local government areas of the country.

The above suggested tremendous quantitative achievement by DFRRI in all areas of the objectives. However, the quality of amenities provided posed a lot of problems, which reduced the impact of the Directorate on the rural communities. Furthermore, considering that there are more than 97, 000 rural communities in Nigeria, these achievements were far from being adequate to solve the problems of rural life in the country. Some other problems which DFRRI faced was its inability to find a modus vivendi with other executive agencies of government, and ineffective grassroots monitoring and follow-up systems due to the large extent of the areas to be serviced, and the paucity of staff and logistic support.

7. National Directorate of Employment (NDE): This programme came into being during Gen. Ibrahim Babandiga's regime. It was established to deal with the rising unemployment in the country. It was structured to offer job seekers an opportunity of finding employment or working on their own through agriculture, industry and handicrafts. Each participant in the scheme was empowered to find jobs or otherwise to benefit from loans guaranteed by the establishment. NDE had its attendant problems, which included low funding for all participants, poor preparation of job seekers and the application of bureaucratic systems.

8. The National Directorate for Social Mobilization: Gen. Ibrahim Babangida's Administration established the directorate in 1987. It was popularly called Mass Mobilization for Self-reliance and Economic Recovery (MAMSER). It pursued aggressively the mobilization and enlightenment of the people towards their rights and duties. It covered the whole nation appealing to the conscience and sense of responsibility of the people, which is considered a most important aspect of rural development. It also stepped up a virile campaign for food production through its *Food First Programme*.

9. The Better Life Programme: Following the outcome of Beijing Conference of 1985, Chief (Mrs.) MaryamBabangida initiated the Better Life Programme for Rural Women in September 1987. The objectives of the programme, according to Obasi and Oguche (1995), include:

- to stimulate and motivate rural women towards achieving better living standards, and sensitize the rest of Nigerians to their problems;
- to educate rural women on simple hygiene, family planning, the importance of child-care and increased literacy rates;
- to mobilize women collectively in order to improve their general lot and for them to seek and achieve leadership roles in all spheres of society;
- to raise consciousness about their rights, the availability

of opportunities and facilities, their social, political and economic responsibilities;
- to encourage recreation and enrich family life; and
- to inculcate the spirit of self-development particularly in the fields of education, business, the arts, crafts and agriculture (pp.74 – 75).

The activities of the Belter Life Programme were remarkable to the extent that its impact was felt throughout the length and breadth of the country. Some of the achievements of Better Life Programme included that:

i. It exposed the potentials of women in creativity and management.

ii. Women became actively involved in all government programmes from the grassroots.

iii. Credit and other inputs now flow to rural organizations more than ever before.

iv. It had the establishment of ministries of women affairs in all the states of the federation (Ijere, 1990: 59).

PROBLEMS AFFECTING RURAL DEVELOPMENT IN NIGERIA

Ijere (1990) remarked that rural development will continue to be a basic problem to developing countries including Nigeria, because of the following reasons:

1. Lack of National Philosophical Base. The Nigerian rural development strategy lacked a philosophical, ideological and holistic foundation. It had a body (policy-makers and government functionaries) but had no soul to give it life and sense of direction. The usual practice has been to be in office propounding slogans and manifestations for the people below. That was instrumental to the failure of some rural development projects such as Farm Settlement Scheme, Operation Feed the Nation, Green Revolution, etc. A philosophical base is typified by an internal motivating and compelling force or commitment stemming from faith and love of the sapiens in the rural sector and determination to work for their upliftment. Without philosophical super structure, rural development remains an echo of good intentions from government and urban dwellers.

2. Lack of Integrated Pilot Demonstration. Before 1976, there was no national rural development programme in Nigeria.

What was in vogue was segmented or unco-ordinated rural development where it is assumed that new programmes in one community will have ripple effects on other communities and institutions. According to Oyaide ((1988), the first Department of Rural Development at federal level was established in 1976 to mobilize people, initiate local projects with local leadership, promote agriculture, rural development and community projects. By 1978, the government was not so sure of what to do with rural development. As such, the term "rural development" was added to the Federal Ministry of Agriculture, and later replaced with Water Resources. All these occur because it is not certain about the place of rural development in the overall development strategy.

3. Lack of Cohesive Identity. Failures have occurred in rural development as people regard the social and cultural aspects of development as subordinate to the economic development. Any innovation that does not guarantee the cohesiveness of the group and respect for their history and beliefs have little hope of survival.

4. Defective Local Economies. People tend to treat rural development projects as charity or welfare packages. Few people are interested in the costing, evaluating and ensuring that targets are met. As such, production is emphasized in rural development policy while marketing and marketing outlets are neglected. For example, Kano State Government in 1983 poured in a huge amount of money (about ₦ 895 million) into Kano River Basin Agricultural Project with little or nothing to show for them on the ground.

5. Lack of Core Project Leadership. The failure of project leadership to come from within to sustain the development projects has led to the falling apart of things in rural development. The tendency has been to rely on official leadership for carrying out rural projects. These official leaders are not prepared to motivate and sustain the enthusiasm of the people in the face of conflicts, depressions and unfulfilled expectations.

6. Inadequate Community Participation. The top-bottom approach to rural development employed by government functionaries whip up enthusiasm among the people, as there is absence of total community participation. Due to the approach adopted, people evoke unwilling response as they are regarded as being incapable of standing on their feet.

7. Lack of Grassroots Planning. There is little or no attempt to allow the rural communities to identify the problems and goals, analyze their own needs, and commit themselves to the achievement of targets. Local experts, Chiefs and community leaders, were taken for granted in deciding what projects to embark upon, and where and how to execute them. The planners do not consult even the interest groups, the co-operatives, and professional organizations.

8. Inability to Optimize Local Resources. Due to Nigeria's penchant for foreign-made goods, local resources are neglected for the imported goods. Local talents and manpower as well as other resources are also ignored, thereby loosing the opportunity of evolving appropriate technology.

9. Neglect of Community Structural Approach. The pattern in Rural Development Programmes in Nigeria centres on the imposition of imported schemes whether or not they are related to the cultural and sociological life of the people. Examples of these areas of neglect include: appointing new leaders where such leaders already exist, not making use of youth organizations, age grades and women's groups in the initiation and implementation of programmes.

THE WAY FORWARD

It has been observed that all the government's efforts on rural development have as their primary aim, improvement of food, cash crops and agricultural production. However, the truth of the matter is that rural development is more comprehensive than agricultural development. This is because; agricultural development simply aims at increasing farm yield, whether for consumption, for industries or for export. Therefore, while agricultural development could increase the economic prosperity of the rural people (dwellers), the experience so far shows that it was more for the benefits of others (especially, urban dwellers). It is susceptible to exploitation. Therefore, the idea of rural transformation should be adopted. Rural transformation involves comprehensive, all-round structural and fundamental changes not just in the physical conditions of the rural inhabitants but more so in the mental, physiological, as well as cultural aspect of development. Rural development is the total development of the rural people which, to be genuine and lasting, has to be affected by their own efforts. It has to go beyond employment generation, equitable distribution of income, widespread improvement in health, nutrition and housing, creation of incentives and opportunities for savings, credit and investments, increased assess to educational facilities, etc. Yet, as comprehensive as these indices of rural development are, they still fall short of the scope of rural transformation. Rural transformation takes as given, the entire political, economic and socio-cultural structure of the rural people as they are.

Rural transformation involves a highly political concept that centres not only on the redistribution of present wealth, but also on a total re-location of political power. The target of rural transformation is the culture of the people. So, transformation in this context goes beyond infrastructural development to super-structural development. Therefore, the hard and core of rural transformation is political empowerment, restructuring of the power relations between the urban and the rural, as well as between the rural and the national interest to which the former (rural area) has always been perpetually sacrificed. The objectives of rural transformation include:

- ❖ to improve the quality of life of the rural people so that they would enjoy desired wants, and would want to stay where they are.
- ❖ to promote more equitable distribution of public investments between the rural and urban areas so as to instill in the rural people a sense of hope, confidence, and self-determination.
- ❖ to make the rural environment so healthy and attractive as to trigger off a reverse the voluntary rural-urban migration among the present urban refugees.
- ❖ to provide opportunity for the rural people to express their political awareness and restructure their traditional relationship and stereotypic mutual attitudes of urban and rural dwellers.
- ❖ to enhance the production of food and industrial raw materials for national development.

The strategies for sustainable rural development in Nigeria, according to Eboh (1995) include the following:

- investing in human development to alleviate rural poverty, human misery and stabilize populations;
- ensuring food security (not just food-sufficiency) through rural compensation measures like selective poverty-targeted

relief;
- creating incentives for rural growth and employment by improving access to production resources and institutional services;
- empowering rural people via participatory and community-oriented development that is woven around local principles, skills and technologies, and
- protecting the environment by generating and facilitating appropriate resource management systems (pp. 8 – 9).

Based on the fore-going, Ogbazi (2006) states that the programme of action in rural transformation as contained in the objectives of the National Policy on Rural Development should include the following:

a. Adequate Supply of Infrastructural Facilities: The government's efforts should aim at raising the standard of living of the rural people through adequate inter-village communication such as good road network, electricity, pipe-borne water, recreational facilities, etc. Government should avoid cultural invasion on the rural people.

b. Provision of Small and Medium-scale Industries: Government should stimulate rural industries, which must be based on rural raw materials available in that area. The small and medium-scale enterprises will turn out goods that will feed the urban and suburban-based industries. Such rural-based industries must be essentially labour-intensive rather than capital-intensive since the required manpower must be indigenous and appropriate. It will therefore create large employment opportunity for rural youths. In doing so, the economic sector will be improved, and the youths would stay and develop their rural environment.

c. Formation of Co-operative Societies: The formation of co-operatives eliminates the fat middlemen, and asserts the rights of the peasant farmers to negotiate the prices of their own product. It could help in checking the new spectre of exploitation by giving a voice to the farmers in the determination of the prices of their own goods.

d. Political Empowerment of the Rural People: The government must make politics to go beyond paternalistic decentralization of power to the lower community. The traditional relationship and the stereotypic mutual attitudes of urban and rural dwellers must be restructured. The *silentmajority,* who are subject to deceptions and exploitations by the city demagogues, should be given opportunity to express their political awareness. They should be rid of their ignorance of political clout and illiteracy, which both conspired to rob the rural people of the realization of their power to change things around to their own advantage. The rural people should be encouraged to form discussion groups to articulate their problems and try to solve them inevitably. Efforts should be made to keep them abreast on government's activities through the establishment of radio-listening and television-viewing centres.

CONCLUSION

In all ramifications, development is for the people and therefore must be designed to meet their needs. This means that all rural development efforts must be derived from the felt-needs and aspirations of the rural people and not in response to the needs of the urban political economy such as unemployment, food shortfalls and rural-urban migration. The present rural development situation poses great problems to all and sundry. Government should show the necessary leadership by matching words with action through evolving workable rural development approaches, proper co-ordination, funding and technical assistance. It should also encourage nation's experts to make useful contributions with their talents. Government has a chief role of building and financing an enduring political, social, cultural and environmental structure on which rural development can thrive, through the encouragement and recognition of the roles of cooperatives, NGOs, and private initiatives as their grass-roots' appeals promote sustainable rural development. This paper strongly recommends the need for government to concentrate its efforts to the encouragement of private initiatives, teaching and propagation of cooperative philosophy and peaceful coexistence to the rural dwellers as education forms the bedrock for rural development. This means that more opportunities should be given to the rural people for participation in decisions that govern their lives. Therefore, proper human capital development should be developed and maintained so as to eliminate the paternalistic view which assumes that the rural people are passive and fatalistic, uninterested in improvement of their lives, and incapable of making initiatives for improvement.

REFERENCES

Afigbo, A. E. (1991). Women as a factor in development.In M. O. Ijere (Ed.); *Women in NigerianEconomy.* Enugu: ACENA Publishers.

Ayichi.D. (1995). Models of rural development in Nigeria: with special focus on the ADPs. In E. C. Eboh, C. U. Okoye and D. Ayichi (Eds.); *Rural Development in Nigeria: Concepts, Processes and Prospects.* Enugu: Auto-Century Publishing Company.

Eboh, E. C. (1995). Sustainable development: the theory and implications for rural Nigeria. In E. C. Eboh.C. U. Okoye and D. Ayichi (Eds.); *Rural Development in Nigeria: Concepts, Processes and Prospects.* Enugu: Auto-Century Publishing Company.

Ekpo, A. H. and Olaniyi, O. (1995). Rural development in Nigeria: analysis of the impact of the Directorate for Food, Roads and Rural Infrastructure (DFRRI) 1986 - 93. In E. C. Eboh, C. U. Okoye and D. Ayichi (Eds.); *Rural Development in Nigeria: Concepts, Processes and Prospects.* Enugu: Auto-Century Publishing Company.

Federal Republic of Nigeria (1981).*Third National Development Plan.* Lagos.

Hunter, G. (1964). *The New Societies of Tropical Africa.* New York: Frederick A. Praeger.

Igbokwe, E. M. and Ajala, A. A. (1995).Popular participation for rural development in Nigeria. In E. C. Eboh, C. U. Okoye and D. Ayichi (Eds.); *Rural Development in Nigeria: Concepts, Processes and Prospects.* Enugu: Auto-Century Publishing Company.

Ijere, M. O. (1990). The challenges of rural development in Nigeria. In A. I. Ikeme (Ed.); *The Challenges of Agriculture in National Development.* Enugu: Optimal Computer Solutions, Ltd.

Ijere, M. O. (1992). *Leading Issuesin Rural Development.* Enugu: ACENA Publishers.

Lele, U. and Adu-Nyako, K. (1991). Integrated strategy approach for poverty alleviation: a paramount priority for Africa. *African Development Review.* 3 (1); 1 – 29.

Obasi, I. N. and Oguche, D. (1995). Innovative programmes in rural development in Nigeria: an evaluation of the Better Life Programme using the APBS framework. In E. C. Eboh, C. U. Okoye and D. Ayichi (Eds.); *Rural Development in Nigeria: Concepts, Processes and Prospects.* Enugu: Auto-Century Publishing Company.

Ogbazi, N. J. (2006). The Role of Agricultural Education in Rural Development. In E. E. Umebali and C. J. C. Akuibilo.(Eds.); *Readings in Cooperative Economics and Management.* Lagos: Computer Edge Publishers.

Ogidefa, I. (2010). Rural development in Nigeria: concept, approaches, challenges and prospect.
http://socyberty.com/issues/rural-development-in-nigeria-concept-approaches-challenges-and-prospcct/.Retrieved on March 22, 2010.

Okorie, A. and Umezurike, C. A. C. (1990). Nigerian agricultural policies: a review. In A. I. Ikeme (Ed.); *The Challenges of Agriculture in National Development.* Enugu: Optimal Computer

SolutionsLtd.

Osuntogun, S. and Olufokunbi, L. C. (1986).History and assessment of agricultural policies in Nigeria.In S. Osuntogun and E. Ugorji (Eds.); *Financing Agricultural development in Nigeria.*llorin: ARMTI Seminar Series; Nov.

Otoghagua, E. (1999). I960 – 2003 Profile of Nigeria Heads of Slate Achievements and Failures.*Benin City: Redemption International Company.*

Oyaide, O. F. (1988). Rural development in Nigeria: the role of government. *Centre for Rural Development and Co-operative (CROC) Lecture Series,* University of Nigeria; February 29.

Williams, S. K. T. (1994). Issues and priority in agricultural extension in Nigeria in the 21st century.*Keynote Address Presented at the Maiden Conference of Society for Nigerian Agricultural Extension.* ARMTI, llorin, February 28 – March 4

ABOUT THE AUTHOR

Ugwuaku Ogechukwu Virginia

Ugwuaku Ogechukwu Virginia holds a Bachelor of Education degree in Adult Education/Administration from the prestigious University of Nigeria, Nsukka.

BOOKS BY THIS AUTHOR

The E-Book Publishing Guide

This book is a guide to easy eBook publishing on an Amazon Account

www.ingramcontent.com/pod-product-compliance
Lightning Source LLC
Chambersburg PA
CBHW072237230526
45466CB00024B/2084